Jean Georges d'Hoste

Les BAUX-DE-PROVENCE

80 Colour illustrations

© Copyright by
CASA EDITRICE BONECHI
Via Cairoli 18/b - 50131 Firenze - Italia
Tel. +39 055 576841 - Fax +39 055 5000766
E-mail: bonechi@bonechi.it
Internet: www.bonechi.it

Team work. All rights reserved.
No part of this publication may be reproduced
or transmitted in any form or by any means,
electronic, chemical or mechanical,
including photocopying, recording, or
by any information storage and retrieval
system, without permission in writing
from the publisher.
The cover, layout and artwork by the
Casa Editrice Bonechi *graphic artists*
in this publication are protected
by international copyright.

Printed in Italy by
Centro Stampa Editoriale Bonechi.

Translated by Susan Fraser.

ISBN 88-7009-385-9

* * *

*On approaching Les Baux, one immediately encounters these two magnificent chimneys built one on top of the other; they were used to heat the large rooms in part of the Maison du Roy which has since been demolished.
Below: in front of the chimneys, a quiet corner around a column crowned by a cross.
Following page: Maison du Roy which is now used as the Post Office.*

In Les Baux, the sun reigns supreme, casting its rays over that region, every inch of which has been jealously guarded since time immemorial; it is the same beauty that other warriors tried to snatch away from its original inhabitants by means of long sieges, raids and pitched battles. It would have cost less in terms of human lives and suffering if they had said, "Let's divide up the rich countryside surrounding Les Baux", but the time was not yet ripe. Nowadays, Les Baux throws open its door to tourists, lovers of authentic beauty and artists, who will never cease to abound in the vicinity. It opens its door with an alluring invitation, "Enter. Take your fill of our treasures whose recollection will fill you with joy".

The French historian, Georges Duby, stated: "When we think of the perfect accomplishment of the human being, his freedom and happiness, we always have the Mediterranean in mind. In fact, all hinterland peoples have always dreamt of the Mediterranean since the dawn of history". In fact, we can still see them today, no longer waging war but peacefully invading the Mediterranean basin from the rocky inlets of Greece to Gibraltar, soaking up the sun and sea air and assimilating the art and traditions, before leaving for their dark, foggy countries of origin.

The Ligurians top the long list of invaders to set-

Above and on the following page: in the dark, narrow alleys, countless workshops offer local handicrafts.

tle in this region. Known in ancient times as the *Salyans*, they invaded the hinterland and organized themselves in small confederated kingdoms, generally situated in an *oppidum*. The Greek geographer Strabone, born in 58 B.C., described certain characteristics of these people. For instance, they used "to hang the heads of enemies defeated in battle around their horses' necks and take them home where they attached them above their entrances". Diodorus, another Greek historian at the time of Augustus, who travelled widely before settling in Rome, went as far as to say that "some of them would have refused to exchange these heads for their weight in gold, demonstrating their pride in being barbarians". Hardy sailors and intrepid warriors, the Romans had a hard time defeating them later on before managing to enforce their law upon them. In approximately 1000 B.C., the Ligurians occupied the town, jostling the peoples who had settled there since ancient times; but this entire little world was to be subjected to peaceful relationships interspersed by the outbursts of anger of the various tribes. With their occupation, the first fortresses appeared: oppidums surrounded by moats behind which the inhabitants could take refuge if need be. As from the Iron Age (starting from 450 B.C.), Celts from southern Germany invaded the region. The Celtic

*Above: the buildings along the Grande-Rue featured cellars to store foodstuffs in the event of a siege.
Following page: at the corner of Jean de Brion Palace (XVI century) stands a tower decorated with elegant windows.*

civilization ended with the dark years that preceded Christianity, making room for the Gallo-Romans, descendants of the Roman and Celtic civilizations whose origins date back to approximately 120 B.C. and who were conquered by the Barbarians (about the Vth century A.D.). This rich civilization left behind the Aurelia Way linking Rome to Arelate (Arles) and to Les Baux. Further findings: the "Trémaïé", a pagan sculpture "adopted" by the Christian religion who saw in it the representation of the Maries, who Three ended up not far from there and the "stèle des Gaïé" indicating a tomb-stone erected by a son in honour and memory of his parents.

Shortly before 500 A.D., Euric (ca. 420-484), king of the Visigoths, covered the region with his hordes, intent on conquering Provence and part of Spain. Believers in the doctrine of Arius who denied Christ's divinity, they destroyed all property belonging to the early Christians. However, Euric's son, Alaric II, was defeated and killed by Clovis in 507 at the Battle of Voillé, making way for the *Regnum Francorum*, which was to suffer the terrible raids of the Lombards (569), Visigoths (87) and Arabs (725) before being attached to Charlemagne's empire. The great emperor's shadow did not prevent the Saracen and Norman incursions; one got the impression that all peoples

Above: Manville Palace at the corner of rue du Château and rue des Fours.
Below: a picturesque street near Manville Palace.
Following page: Hôtel de Manville, built in about 1571. The tricolour indicates that it is the town hall. Its interior is lavishly decorated.

Following pages: the noteworthy windows marked with a cross of the Hôtel de Manville and a window opening of the building adjacent to Hôtel de Manville in rue Nueve. Under the architrave, one can read the saying «Post tenebras lux 1571».

Above: this Medieval building nowadays houses a typical Provençal workshop. Below: interior of a shop where they sell the famous herbs of Provence used to perfume linen and kitchenware.
Following page: at a street corner, a poetical view with a charming bell.

Above: old, winding roads.
Below: situated between Hôtel Des Porcelets and the Church of St Vincent, this Gothic tower was, according to legend, originally a lantern in memory of the dead.
Following page: the house called Hôtel des Porcelets (XVI century) with its severe façade adorned by a window divided into panels.

The church of St Vincent (XII century) with its square bell-tower, considerably renovated during the sixteenth century.

Above and on page 20: the seventeenth century chapel of the «Pénitents Blancs» on Saint-Vincent Square. Above the portal in rustic work, two kneeling penitents flank a partly mutilated ornamental motif. It houses a magnificent fresco by the great Provençal artist, Yves Brayer.

On page 21: this old sixteenth century chepel, whose façade was restored during the following century, housed the municipal offices before being used as the Museum of «Santons», typical figures in Provençal mangers. Below: the road penetrates into the rock-face.

MUSEE DES SANTONS

Four pictures of the road leading to the castle.

The Lapidarian Museum exhibits archaeological and architectural finds from the castle. On the following two pages, views of the castle.

of the ancient and pre-Medieval worlds had it at heart to pass over this land, dominating it and fertilizing it with their blood before being chased away by new conquerors.

Provence is the result of these mixtures of peoples who came from far and wide and these complicated entanglements under the benevolent gaze of the sun.

After Charlemagne, Provence changed its ruler, but did it ever have a ruler? The Carolingian times were troubled and uncertain with the struggle for power between the Church and State. Through complicated successions, difficult to trace, power was handed to Lothaire, Charlemagne's grandson, who divided his states between his children in 855; Charles was given Provence which then passed into the hands of Louis II the German, his daughter and so forth. The village of Les Baux was virtually left out of these political struggles and awaited its first landed gentry who have been traced back to 950. Authority was placed in the hands of the *Viguier* of Arles who governed in the name of the king of Provence. That is how we find a Pons I, a Pons the Elder and a Pons the Younger handing down power from father to son and administering Les Baux. Hugues I, son of the latter, seems to have been the first real lord of Les Baux and the first to have commissioned a fortress to be built.

Quarrels, jealousy and attraction of that beautiful

In the centre: at the exit to rue du Trencat stands a massive square tower belonging to the fourteenth century palace which originally belonged to the de la Tour du Brau family, now the seat of the Lapidarian Museum.

St Blaise, which was the chapel of the carders and weavers, dates back to the XII century, Below, the entrance to the castle.

part of Provence unleashed the Baussenque wars; two brothers-in-law fought over Provence: Raimond Béranger, the Count of Barcelona and husband of Douce de Gévaudan, and Raymond des Baux or del Balz, husband of Etiennette de Provence, Douce's sister. These wars lasted from 1142 and 1162 and one can imagine the devastation that they caused.

"A l'asar, Bautesard" became the motto of the lords of Les Baux. "Au hasard, Balthazar" was linked to one of the three Wise Men and the star of Bethlehem with sixteen silver rays on a red background is the coat-of-arms. This star - such a "peaceful" element of heraldry when one considers the lions, eagles, griffons, serpents and other monsters of all kinds that often appear - was, perhaps, a vague ray of hope in a stormy sky. Finally, a lineage came to power and died out with the little Alix des Baux, daughter of Raymond II, who died in 1372. Her grandfather, Guillaume de Turenne, whose daughter married Raymond II, became the child's guardian but he expected the Fortress of Baux in return. Odon de Villars, who married Alix in 1380, waged war against the bloodthirsty Guillaume de Turenne, defeating him and recovering his wife's property in 1426. But a new uncertain epoch was initiated because in the absence of direct heirs, Alix made

The noteworthy ruins of the old hospital give an idea of the vastness of the complex originally commissioned by the Manville family. Below, an evocative partial view of the entrance to the old hospital built during the XVI century by order of Jeanne de Quiqueran.

A panoramic view of the fertile countryside near Les Baux.

her will in favour of the Dukes of Andria, distant cousins who had settled in the Naples area. Her will was contested and the following year the fief of Les Baux was transformed into a barony annexed to the County of Provence under the authority of King René d'Anjou, who handed over this land to his second wife, Jeanne de Laval, in 1459.

Queen Jeanne was interested in the arts and enchanted by the landscape of Les Baux. She made countless improvements to the town, evidence of which can still be seen. On the death of the king in 1480, Provence passed into the hands of her nephew, Charles du Maine, who bequeathed that, on his death which occurred the following year, this lovely sunny province was to be handed over to the King of France, Louis XI, who had upheld him in the assertion of his rights.

The inhabitants of Les Baux never felt the same way about Louis XI as they had done about Queen Jeanne! An uprising was thwarted by Jean de Baudricourt's seizure of the castel. He was then named governor of the town and a prudent administration managed to calm the waters; on

Crops in the Crau Valley area and the rocky crag on which the Saracen Tower rises.
On the following page: the imposing lime-stone rock eroded by the wind into a shape reminiscent of various animal forms.

the other hand, the kings of France were powerful and the inhabitants of the old fief preferred to fall into line.
Several famous governors, whose names are reminiscent of glory, such as Anne de Montmorency (1483-1567), constable of France who took part in all the wars and diplomatic feats of the time and was the first adviser to François I, Catherine de' Medici and her son, Charles IX; under this brilliant leader, Les Baux developed considerably. But at this point Montmorency left for new destinations, leaving the town in the hands of Claude de Manville. Before turning the page on the constable, let us recall that in Les Baux he received François I accompanied by his son and by the king of Navarre. Claude de Manville, who was in charge of the town, was no novice: prison captain and sea captain, he became Governor of Les Baux and ardently opposed the Reformation. His son, who took over from him, was in favour and the Protestants settled near to their protector, not without causing uneasiness in the town.

An unusually eroded rock defies the gusts of the mistral. The caves dug into the lime-stone have been given imaginative names by the locals: the Bat, the Black Sheep...

Another governor of great standing was Jean de Quiqueran, who, however, was assassinated in 1563. It was his wife, Jeanne, who had the Pavilion known as the "Pavillon de la Reine Jeanne" erected.

Subsequently, Jean de Manville, another member of the family in favour of the Reformation and Governor of Les Baux, had a small Protestant temple built alongside the family palace in 1571; there are still traces of it in an inscription placed under a window frame: *Post tenebras, lux 1571* (After darkness, light).

The Protestants did not benefit from their freedom of worship for any length of time. In 1618 Jean de Boches and Jacques de Verassy persecuted the Protestants who naturally took refuge in the precincts of the Manvilles; the city was shaken by skirmishes and acts of tyranny. Finally, Louis XIII enforced peace in 1621; however, it was not long-lasting as the inhabitants were in favour of a rebellion against the king headed by his brother, the Duc d'Orléans.

On this and the following pages: man has exploited the imposing rocky crags created by nature to built defence postings in an age in which the region was exposed to the passing of armies whose intents were not always peaceful.

On this and the following pages: the ruins of the castle evoke the strength and elegance of architectural lines of the original building. Even though there is no sign of life, a fallen arch, crumbling steps and a deserted pigeon loft do not instill a sense of nostalgia and sadness in onlookers because Provence, land of passion, manages to drive melancholy away.

Louis XIII and Richelieu were accustomed to these towns rising up against royal authority, but they also knew how to suppress them. In 1627-1628 La Rochelle fell out of favour with the king when it opted for an alliance with the English. Completely devastated by hunger and disease, it was forced to surrender, accepting the severe conditions dictated by the sovereign. Charles d'Estoublon, Governor of Arles, was charged with taking the town by storm and it was forced to surrender after a siege lasting twenty days. The king and Charles d'Estoublon entered into negotiations to reach an agreement that was satisfactory to both parties. The citadel, which had been stormed so many times and whose walls had withheld so many ferocious attacks, was razed to the ground; furthermore, its archives went up in flames and the imposing fortifications with their sun-kissed towers were knocked down. As a token gesture of their renouncement to any further uprisings, the townsfolk were entitled to reacquire their freedom from the king by paying a huge

Ruins of a chapel from which fervent, humble prayers rose to invoke heavenly protection, like countless, anonymous tongues of flame in the vortex in the history of humanity.

Such magnificent ruins could arouse in each one of us the vocation to become an archeologist, historian or researcher. Is it a palace, a private home or a chapel? Or the remains of a well? The mind boggles, yet the stones keep their secret. Isn't this a welcome change in a rational world in which there is very little left to the immagination.

sum. An agreement was reached but the walls gradually crumbled. There were not sufficient funds for the enormous undertaking, to pay the king and to re-establish a semblance of local economy that enabled them to survive. In 1639, the town asked the king to release them from their debt and finally form part of the crown lands. The first marquis of Les Baux was Hercule Grimaldi, prince of Monaco; Louis XIII handed over Les Baux to him in 1641 to recompensate him for having driven away the Spanish garrison that had occupied Monaco since 1605. The town of Les Baux then belonged to the Grimaldis until Honoré III (1733-1795) who lost his French possessions under the pressure of the Revolution.

After 1791, calm returned to this centre which, having turned it back on the agitations of its stormy, destructive past, looked resolutely towards a promising future, thanks to its first class hotels which only add to the pleasure of a visit.

Wandering through these crumbling fortresses, at each step one discovers the remains of columns, arches and rooms whose origins have been forgotten and where troubadours used to sing about the beauty of some beloved while playing the violin.

The town of Les Baux belongs to a deep-rooted ethnic group: Languedoc. It boasts a glorious past, original traditions, an autochtonous culture and its own language.

As from the XIth century, *Langue d'oc* spread like wild fire to the entire region now occupied by southern France. Given the vastness of the territory, various dialects cropped up such as Gascon, Limousin, and Provençal Languedoc dialects. For five centuries *Langue d'oc* poets - the famous troubadors - popularized their flourishing literature, which had considerable repercussions on northern French, Italian and Spanish literature, not to mention *Minnesänger*, the German minstrels. The term is derived from *trobar* which in *Langue d'oc* means poetic bent.

The names of 460 troubadours were documented at the end of the Fourteenth Century. This vast number gives us an idea of the creativity and wealth of literature at the time. The favourite themes of this

The ruins of the castle, once occupied by the noblemen of Les Baux. Pope Clement VII and King François I sojourned here.

cultural circle, dedicated above all to celebrate *courtly love* were unrequited love for a damsel, sometimes identified as the Virgin Mary or for an imaginary princess from a remote land. Reference is also made to the Crusades and to chivalry and we frequently find invectives against French invaders and the clergy.

The troubadours, who included some women known as *trobairitz*, belonged to all social classes and generally lived at the court of some powerful lord where they were highly respected or passed from one castle to the other and livened up long vigils with their songs. In fact theirs was a sung, lyrical poetry and only in certain cases was it put to music.

However, notwithstanding the flourishing of their literature, their language went into a decline at the end of the XIIIth century. Gradually royal offices from northern France tried to enforce French, that then became the language of the notables.

At the time of Louis XIV and during the following centuries, Langue d'oc with its rich shades of meaning was considered a dialect spoken by the lower classes and by the peasants. An attempt to resuscitate Langue d'oc culture took place in Mar-

From the top of the castle, one has a excellent view over the rocks of the Valley of Hell which, according to legend, inspired Dante for the Divine Comedy, and over the Valley of the Crau, as far as the sea.

On the following page: the mighty walls of Les Baux seem to emerge as if by magic from the rocks.

A walk along the ancient walls which wind along the rocky crags covered in lichen brings back to mind the era of battles and sieges.

All that remains of the tower of Les Baux, demolished by Louis XI, are pieces of walls with fine window openings.

Monument to the Provençal poet, Charles Rieu.

A last glimpse of the rock of Les Baux before ending our tour of this landscape and unusual buildings that lets the imagination run wild.

seille in 1851; Joseph Roumanille had *Li Prouvençalo* (The Provençals) by various authors, including Théodore Aubanel and Fréderic Mistral, published. On 21st May 1854, a group of seven Provençal poets founded *Félibrige*, a movement aiming at the rebirth of Langue d'oc literature and the purification of the language which had become corrupted with the passing of time. It was Mistral, one of the seven founder poets, who gave it the name *félibre* (hence Félibrige) to the Provençal writers. He took the word from a song that narrated the story of Jesus in the Temple with the seven doctors in law (*li sèt félibre de la lei*). After some years the movement became organized, promulgated a statute, founded local schools and created four *maintenances* (Provence, Languedoc, Aquitaine and Catalonia) presided over by *majorau* who in turn elected the *capoulié* or great master of Félibrige. This group produced some literary masterpieces: *Mirèio* (1859) by Mistral and the following year the delightful *Miougrano entreduberto* (The half-closed pomegranate) by Aubanel.

The peasant poet Charloun Rieu (1846-1924), born in Paradou, was a direct descendant of these troubadours and was elected as head of the assembly of Fébrilige in 1910. His book entitled *Li Cant dou Terrair* (Songs of my land), highly poetical and original, was very successful. Furthermore, he translated the Odyssey into Provençal.

Les Baux-de-Provence

1 - Entrée actuelle
2 - Maison du Roy
3 - Maison de Brion
4 - Hôtel de Manville
5 - Hôtel des Porcelets (Musée des Baux)
6 - Eglise Saint-Vincent
7 - Chapelle des Pénitents Blancs
8 - Hôtel de la Tour du Brau (Musée lapidaire)
9 - Chapelle Saint-Blaise
10 - Ancien hôpital
11 - Monument Charloun Rieu
12 - Ancien rempart
13 - Chapelle Sainte-Catherine
14 - Ancien château
15 - Pigeonnier
16 - Donjon
17 - Tour sarrasine